LIKE A

Summer Peach

SUNBRIGHT POEMS &

LIKE A *Summer Peach*

OLD SOUTHERN RECIPES

Edited by

BLANCHE FLANDERS FARLEY

JANICE TOWNLEY MOORE

PAPIER-MACHE PRESS
WATSONVILLE, CA

00 99 98 97 96   5 4 3 2 1

ISBN: 0-918949-89-0 Hardcover

Cover and interior fabric-and-thread images © by Deidre Scherer
Cover and interior design by Linda Criswell
Text composition by Linda Criswell
Editors' photograph by Alvin Townley, Jr.
Proofreading by Erin Lebacqz
Interior graphics by Rick Thomson

Note: The publisher has not tested the recipes in this publication, and thereby specifically disclaims any liability related to the publication or use of these recipes, nor is the publisher responsible for any claims or causes of action alleged to have arisen from the use or replication of any of the recipes or ingredients listed, or for any mistake, whether a misstated or allegedly incorrect instruction.

Library of Congress Cataloging-in-Publication Data

Like a summer peach : sunbright poems and old Southern recipes / edited by
    Blanche Flanders Farley and Janice Townley Moore.
            p. cm.
        ISBN 0-918949-89-0 (hardcover : alk. paper)
        1. Food—Poetry. 2. American poetry—20th century. 3. Cookery,
    American—Southern style.   I. Farley, Blanche Flanders. II. Moore,
    Janice Townley.
    PS595.F65L55 1996
    8ll'.54080355—dc20
                                                    96-72
                                                    CIP

FOR OUR TWO FAVORITE COOKS

Martha Lake Flanders

Edith Davis Townley

Contents

3   Appetite—*Maxine Kumin*

4   Raspberries in Cream

5   Love Poem at a Particular Breakfast for
       No Particular Woman—*John Stone*

6   Muffin-Morning Blueberry Muffins

7   Preserves—*Michael Waters*

8   Raspberry (or Blackberry) Preserves

8   Easy "Scratch" Biscuits

9   Saturday Morning—*Steven Harvey*

10   Martha Candler Lee's Waffles

11   Salsa Omelette for Two

12   Julia Child's Duck—*Janice Townley Moore*

14   Sustenance—*Judson Mitcham*

15   Garden Fresh Vegetable Soup

16   Corn Sticks

17   Afterward—*Judy Goldman*

19   Split Pea Soup

20   Vegetable Market: Trying to Talk with a Friend
       —*Mary Ann Coleman*

21   Eggplant Incognito

21   her sure hand—*Peggy Lyles*

22   Eating Small Birds—*Sarah Gordon*

23   Vegetarian Spaghetti

25   Potatoes—*Kathryn Stripling Byer*

26   Confetti Potato Salad

27   Soufflé—*Blanche Flanders Farley*

28   Sweet Potato Soufflé

29	Your Poems Have Been Lost in the Mail —*Memye Curtis Tucker*
30	Crunchy Sweet Potato Chips
31	Homage to a Cook—*Rena G. Patton*
32	Family Reunion Chicken 'n Dumplings
32	old homeplace...—*Peggy Lyles*
33	Sea Oats—*Bettie Sellers*
34	Shrimp Casserole
35	Stew—*Andrea Hollander Budy*
36	Beef Stew for Any Season
36	Mother-daughter—*Peggy Lyles*
37	Tongue-Tied—*Naomi Shihab Nye*
38	Tortillas to Tempt Your Taste Buds
39	Making Bread—*Dorothy Coffin Sussman*
41	Sally Lunn Bread
42	Sponge Cake—*Ann Ritter*
43	Orange Sponge Cake
44	Old Georgia Tea Cakes
44	half a heart shape—*Peggy Lyles*
45	Surfaces—*John Foster West*
46	Aunt Clyde's Chocolate Layer Cake
47	To a Wasp—*Janice Townley Moore*
48	Black Forest Cheesecake ("Lite")
49	Peach Custard Pie
51	Peaches—*Peter Davison*

LIKE A Summer Peach

APPETITE

Maxine Kumin

I eat these
wild red raspberries
still warm from the sun
and smelling faintly of jewelweed
in memory of my father

tucking the napkin
under his chin and bending
over an ironstone bowl
of the bright drupelets
awash in cream

my father
with the sigh of a man
who has seen all and been redeemed
said time after time
as he lifted his spoon

men kill for this.

RASPBERRIES IN CREAM

3 egg whites
½ teaspoon vanilla
½ teaspoon cream of tartar
1 cup sugar
1 cup crushed saltines
½ cup chopped pecans
1 medium container whipped topping
fresh or frozen raspberries

Beat egg whites, vanilla, and cream of tartar until foamy. Gradually add sugar, 2 tablespoons at a time, and beat until stiff peaks form. Combine cracker crumbs and nuts. Fold into egg whites. Spread in a well-greased 9- x 13-inch pan. Bake at 350 degrees F for 30 minutes. Let cool. Cover with whipped topping. Top with sliced raspberries, slightly sweetened, or frozen raspberries, thawed.

Alternate: Use fresh or frozen strawberries.

Love Poem at a Particular Breakfast for No Particular Woman

John Stone

This blueberry muffin
is on its way to becoming
your breast.
It is only partway there,
not nearly far enough,
smaller, harder.

Nothing is perfect.
It is better so. Of course.

But it makes me want
to taste you.

I'd like, some muffin-morning,
to love you like the last movement
of Mozart's 22nd Piano Concerto.

But this blueberry muffin
at breakfast
is as good a place as any
to begin.

MUFFIN-MORNING BLUEBERRY MUFFINS

2 cups all-purpose flour
½ cup sugar
4 teaspoons baking powder
½ teaspoon salt
½ teaspoon baking soda
1 cup milk
1 egg
¼ cup margarine or butter-flavored
    shortening, melted
1 teaspoon vanilla
1 cup blueberries

Wash and drain blueberries. Line muffin tins with paper baking cups. In a large bowl, mix all dry ingredients and set aside. In a small bowl, beat milk, egg, and melted margarine (or shortening). Add vanilla. Blend into dry ingredients just until moistened. Gently fold in blueberries. Fill 12 muffin cups ⅔ to ¾ full. Bake at 400 degrees F for 15 to 18 minutes.

PRESERVES

Michael Waters

I found the preserves in the cellar,
canned decades ago
by the woman who brought this house
on wheels from Missouri.

The black raspberries were still
delicious, each cluster
burning like years in the brain.
I could almost hear the song

used to press those raspberries
into jars thinner, now, than dust,
almost imitate each gesture
as the stain rose on my fingers.

The stuffed owls are crumbling now
like rags left too long in bins,
the black rafters warp—
but the slow spirals of dust

still resist sweeping,
having been written in the journal
of the lost, to keep track
of what passes, what preserves.

RASPBERRY PRESERVES

(OR BLACKBERRY)

3 ½ cups of pulp from berries
1 box fruit pectin
5 cups sugar
2 tablespoons lemon juice

Run approximately 2 quarts of berries through a food mill or sieve to remove seeds and to yield about 3-1/2 cups of pulp. Combine pulp and fruit pectin in a heavy pot. Bring to a hard boil (one that boils almost up to the top of the pan). Add sugar and lemon juice and boil 2 minutes. Dip spoon in jam to test. Jam is done when it does not run off spoon but comes off in droplets. Pour into sterilized jars and seal.

EASY "SCRATCH" BISCUITS

2 cups self-rising flour (sift before measuring)
3 tablespoons vegetable shortening
⅔ cup milk

Cut shortening into flour with pastry blender. Add milk gradually until a soft dough forms. Roll out on floured cloth or board. Bake at 450 degrees F until golden brown.

SATURDAY MORNING

Steven Harvey

Dad musters up a wry, Jackie Gleason smile
and saunters to the stove easing waffles
onto a platter. "Here's the syrup,"
he shouts above the clatter of forks and dishes,
setting the bottle, still dripping, on the table.
"Juice is in the plastic thing over there."

I pour on just enough and a bit more.
Thick dark pools form in waffled crosses,
mixing with butter and turning a streaked brown.
Syrup runs up to the edges, and one
at a time waffled squares spill their sweet cargoes
onto the plate. "Don't play with it!"
Dad scolds.
          "Well he's not, Max,"
Mom interjects,
                    and Dad, shrugging, backs off,
swallowing hard and wiping syrup out of
the corner of his mouth with a napkin.
"Good?" he asks, mouth full, reaching across
the table. "More syrup?"
                    But he's already
pouring it, messing up my careful design,
winning one way or the other.
                              So we eat.
Behind us—charred crumbs, a cluster of forks,
and batter dribbled here and there on the counter
of our linoleum lives.   Mom holds back her hair
as she eats, her mouth in a tight smile,
while a plume of smoke rises to the exhaust fan.

$\mathcal{M}$ARTHA CANDLER LEE'S WAFFLES

2 egg yolks, beaten
2 cups buttermilk
⅓ cup salad oil
2 cups flour
½ teaspoon salt
1 teaspoon baking powder
1 teaspoon baking soda
1 tablespoon sugar
2 egg whites, stiffly beaten

Combine egg yolks, buttermilk, and salad oil. Add flour sifted with salt, baking powder, baking soda, and sugar. Beat well. Fold in egg whites. Bake in hot waffle irons. These are especially good with sliced strawberries and sprinkled with powdered sugar.

$\mathcal{S}$ALSA OMELETTE FOR TWO

3 eggs
3 tablespoons milk
salt and pepper
1 tablespoon oil
1 small tomato, diced
1 shallot, diced
2 tablespoons green bell pepper, chopped
grated cheese
salsa

Beat eggs and milk. Add a dash of salt and pepper.
Heat oil in skillet over low heat. Pour in egg mix-
ture and cook slowly until it begins to set. Using
spatula, lift edges slightly so that bottom portion
will cook evenly. Sprinkle vegetables and cheese
over half of surface. Allow to cook until mixture
seems well set. Fold over, sealing in cheese and
vegetables. Allow to cook approximately 20 sec-
onds. Flip and cook another 20 seconds. Remove
to plate and spread with salsa. Serve immediately.

JULIA CHILD'S DUCK

Janice Townley Moore

In your succulent voice
like gravy in the pan
you convince me
to roast the duck.

But that is not all.
I must try my hand at pâté
from liver and other innards.
The long lean neck
will be stock for soup.

I will make an omelette
from the egg never laid.

SUSTENANCE

Judson Mitcham

We talk about food over the phone.
My mother wants to know if I have eaten,
and I think about the funny old photographs
of babies barely wedged into high chairs, spoons
raised to our round, fat faces
as long as we would swallow,
and we'd swallow until sleep drooped us over.
We talk about white corn, cantaloupe, tomatoes.

In the first year living by herself,
my mother looked starved,
like a refugee in clothes not her own.

This evening, while the soup was on the stove,
I called her, and I told her what was in it:
a sweet Vidalia onion, new potatoes; I detailed
the way I planned to eat it later on—
with the cornbread ready for the oven, mixed
exactly as she taught me. We discussed
the touch of oil added to the cornmeal—how
some varieties are better for the heart—
and then grew quiet. There are times,

like tonight, when the silence we allow
on the telephone holds for us both, I believe,
such a difficult ease, it is almost grace.

GARDEN FRESH VEGETABLE SOUP

2 cans (10½ ounces) chicken broth
2 medium to large onions, chopped
  (Vidalias if possible)
5 or 6 large red ripe tomatoes, peeled (Skins may be
  removed by dropping into boiling water for a
  few minutes. When skins begin to crack, drop
  in cold water and peel.)
2 carrots, sliced
1 pint bag frozen corn, or fresh cut-off
  corn in season
1 16-ounce package assorted frozen vegetables
  (butter beans, beans, etc.)
several pods of okra, sliced
1 small potato, chopped
1 small can tomato sauce
½ teaspoon salt
¼ teaspoon black pepper
1 bay leaf (optional)
1 tiny tip of hot pepper or a few sprinkles of
  cayenne pepper (optional)

Cook all ingredients together except okra and potato. Bring to boil, reduce heat, cover, and simmer for at least 2 hours. Add okra and potato for the last hour.

$\mathcal{C}$ORN STICKS

1 cup plain cornmeal
3 teaspoons baking powder
¾ teaspoon salt
1 large egg
1 tablespoon corn oil
¾ cup milk

Preheat oven and an iron corn stick pan (well greased) to 450 degrees F. Mix cornmeal, baking powder, and salt. Add egg, oil, and milk. Bake about 20 minutes, or until golden brown.

Alternate: Batter may also be baked in an iron skillet.

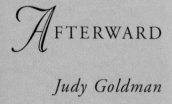FTERWARD

Judy Goldman

The blister of split pea and barley soup,
too thick this time,
too late to add water,
trying to stir,
my wooden spoon coated with swollen pearls,
the potatoes so soft they break into pieces,
carrots, onions, the conversation with you
still simmering, hours old, the way
a simple incident can suddenly clot
and a word or gesture becomes proof
of lack of love, the heat, its hard luster,
everything turning solid
just as hunger sets in.

Split Pea Soup

2 cups dried split peas
2 quarts water
1 ham bone or small shank end of ham
1 medium onion, minced
2 stalks of celery with tops, chopped
2 carrots, thinly sliced
1 sprig fresh parsley
1 small potato, chopped
salt and pepper to taste

Soak peas overnight in water. Add other ingredients and heat to boil. Cook about 2½ hours, or until peas are tender. Season with salt and pepper.

VEGETABLE MARKET: TRYING TO TALK WITH A FRIEND

Mary Ann Coleman

...we sought to find the
first seed once more

George Seferis

Touching eggplant, we admired
the green membrane beneath scratched black skin
glinting purple, tomatoes sealed in satin,
corn in linen husks, pearlescent clusters of spring onions
and broccoli branching like upraised arms.

But you stood naked inside your skull
in a room of mirrors examining the play of images
that moved and flickered as you turned;
Botticelli's Venus reflected in the spume
riding on the shore's edge,
the tiltings of your shoulders caught
and held an instant on the silvered glass.

Then I visited my own inner hall of mirrors,
a crystal palace from an old carnival,
the same glittering side show opening each day.
In the intricate passages, I checked my distorted face
laughing to cover my astonishment
at tricks that flesh and mirrors, coupling, play.
Wanting out, I couldn't see where panels stopped
and space began. My fingers pressed against
the chilling panes. The only exit was the way I came.

We stepped back, slowly, into the vegetable market
and turned to each other. We opened our lips to speak.
But a ray of sun, falling on the narrow aisle
startled the words back into our throats.

We walk home, talking about the weather,
the incredible traffic on Broad Street.

$\mathcal{E}$GGPLANT INCOGNITO

(for people who think they don't like eggplant)

1 medium eggplant
2 onions, chopped
1 tablespoon oil
1 cup whole wheat bread crumbs
¾ cup pecans (or English walnuts),
    chopped
½ teaspoon salt
⅓ cup tomato puree
½ cup sharp cheese, grated

Split eggplant down the middle lengthwise and scoop out pulp, reserving shell. Cook pulp with onions in a small amount of salted water until tender. Drain and mash. Mix cooked vegetables, oil, crumbs, nuts, salt, and puree and fill eggplant shells. Cover with grated cheese and set eggplant in a pan containing ½ inch water. Bake at 375 degrees F for 20 minutes.

her sure hand
with garlic . . .
winter rain

Peggy Lyles

EATING SMALL BIRDS

Sarah Gordon

is for buzzards an indelicate task   for us, a matter of plucking
and cleaning and frying   and sitting down to table
before the footless headless wingless body   brown with batter
seasoned with ancient herbs

is beginning with a leg   pulling it off, gnawing
through sinew and muscle   recalling
Calchas at Aulis   what he said   to bring the winds
to carry the ships   seeing the eagles   destroy the hare
Calchas called for sacrifice   the virgin daughter

is wondering what Audubon   did with the bodies
after he killed them to paint them   to make the books, the catalogs

is saving the breast for last   the softest most succulent bites
closing in on   the meat near the breastbone
chewing carefully   watching for shot   fingers probing, greasy
leaving the thighbones   the backbone   bare

is forgetting what it is we've eaten   missing the head, the heart

VEGETARIAN SPAGHETTI

(the poem on the previous page may inspire you to cook this)

1½ pounds zucchini, thinly sliced
1 bell pepper, chopped
2 stalks celery, chopped
1 large onion, chopped
2 tablespoons olive oil
1 14½-ounce can tomatoes
1 6-ounce can tomato paste
1 2½-ounce jar mushrooms, sliced
1 or 2 cloves of garlic, minced
1 teaspoon salt
¼ teaspoon black pepper
1 bay leaf
spaghetti noodles
Parmesan cheese

Over medium heat, sauté the zucchini, bell pepper, celery, and onion in oil. Add tomatoes, tomato paste, and seasonings. Heat until bubbly. Reduce to low heat, cover, and simmer for a couple of hours. Add mushrooms during last hour. Serve over spaghetti noodles, topped with grated Parmesan cheese.

$\mathscr{P}$OTATOES

Kathryn Stripling Byer

Henry arrives with his rototiller
eager to please. Come March
in the mountains we all want a garden.
We'd grow one in stone
if we had to. But of course
we don't have to. The earth is obliging
and Henry digs rocks from the ground
like a prospector. All afternoon
he plows. Under that jungle
of weeds is good earth. We're surprised.
"Oh, ye farmers of little faith," he laughs
and picks up a brown clod. "Potatoes,"
he says. "I can taste them already.
They'd grow here like grass." The dirt clings
to his fingers. Above our heads
Rocky Face Ridge takes the sun like a lover
and beams. "Good thing
I got this job done today," he says,
rubbing his big palms together
like flint. "Hard rain's coming
tomorrow." Today it is Friday.
Today, I keep saying. Today
and today. We live here
by this patch of plowed earth
and we'll eat potatoes all winter.

CONFETTI POTATO SALAD

4 large Irish potatoes
2 eggs, hard cooked
½ cup celery, chopped
½ cup salad pickles
1 half large green bell pepper, chopped
1 half large red bell pepper, chopped
1 cup mayonnaise
1½ teaspoons prepared mustard
1 teaspoon salt
paprika

Boil potatoes and eggs. Peel and cool several hours in refrigerator. Chop potatoes into cubes and cut up eggs into a large mixing bowl. Add celery, pickles, green and red peppers. In a small bowl, mix mayonnaise, mustard, and salt. Blend into potato mixture. Sprinkle with paprika and refrigerate before serving.

$\mathcal{S}$OUFFLÉ
Blanche Flanders Farley

My daughter gazes out the window as her baby naps.
"Know what I would really like to have?"

I almost guess before she tells me. The sumac's
turning red. September's rapping at her taste buds.
Mine, as well.

So I buy the sweet potatoes—reddish, fat and round,
not stringy—like my mother said to do.
I boil them till the scruffy skin turns smooth,
then cool them down beneath the tap.

My hands become my mother's as I peel, peel back
to that familiar orange hue. I mix and mash. The oven's
hot. A bit of nutmeg. At last, marshmallows, toasting
on the top, swell up like small balloons.

The air is charged with something old and new.
Rooted in our blood, it sings. This is what we wanted,
what my daughter knew. This ancient sweetness
with no strings attached.

SWEET POTATO SOUFFLÉ

3 cups sweet potatoes, cooked and mashed
¾ cup sugar
2 eggs
½ cup milk
½ cup margarine, melted
one bag of large marshmallows

Mix all ingredients except marshmallows and place in buttered casserole. Bake at 350 degrees F for 40 minutes. Remove from oven and cover with large marshmallows. Bake until marshmallows are a golden brown.

YOUR POEMS HAVE BEEN LOST IN THE MAIL

Memye Curtis Tucker

I am not fooled.
Someone is feasting in secret on my words,
crunching my semicolons.
Behind some door he is tasting sounds,
filling himself, image by image.
He holds my lines to the light—
sea mist falls on his tongue.
All night his lips move with stolen dreams,
his lover
tastes my salt.

CRUNCHY SWEET POTATO CHIPS

Peel sweet potatoes and cut into thin slices on cutting board. Cook in large skillet over medium heat in just enough canola oil to cover bottom of skillet until edges are browned. Turn and cook on other side. Drain on paper towels and immediately sprinkle lightly with salt. Serve warm.

HOMAGE
TO A
COOK

Rena G. Patton

You better not mess with Shirley,
especially if you're a vegetarian.
What she puts on the table
every night at seven
is good enough
to cause even you
to eat chicken.

And besides that
she has secret ways
of knowing when
the cabbages up on
Big Scaley are ready.

She's working on an angle
for that cookbook she's got
in mind. You better pray
she doesn't find it, or
she'll be walking
right on out of Rabun County,
Georgia, in those funky Mary Hambidge
socks she wears, loosing
her culinary wiles
on the larger world. But
don't bother calling her,
trying to talk her out of it.
She ain't got no phone.

*F*AMILY REUNION CHICKEN 'N DUMPLINGS

1 hen, cut up (4 to 5 pounds)
salt and pepper
4 cups cake flour
1⅓ cups water
½ cup milk
1 tablespoon butter or margarine

Place chicken in a large pot with enough water to cover.
Season with salt and pepper. Simmer until meat falls from
bones easily. Remove bones. Broth may be strained. In the
meantime prepare dumplings. Add water to cake flour to form
stiff dough. Roll as thin as possible on a lightly floured surface.
Drop by strips into rapidly boiling broth (containing chicken).
Add only one layer at a time. Cover and bring to a boil, and
then add another layer, until all dumplings are used. Cook
covered until tender, about 2 to 4 minutes. Reduce heat and
add milk and butter. Extra salt and pepper may be added.

old homeplace . . .
around the pear tree
fragrant light

Peggy Lyles

EA OATS

Bettie Sellers

The quarter moon cocks its one eye
at sea oats, fragile as rice paper,
holding the Outer Banks
intact against the wind, insistent
from the West this August night.

I have caught it watching me
through the cottage window
as I steep shrimp and rice
in dry vermouth, a feast
to hold against another wind.

Like sea oats holding sand,
this ceremony musical with pots
and pans informs the darkness,
holds it tight around me.
No one is here to sit with me,
wine poured, napkin folded so,
and eat.

$\mathcal{S}$HRIMP CASSEROLE

2 pounds cooked shrimp
1 tablespoon lemon juice
2 tablespoons oil
1 box wild rice mix
½ cup bell pepper, chopped
¾ cup onion, chopped
2 tablespoons butter or margarine
1 teaspoon salt
⅛ teaspoon black pepper
1 can tomato soup
1 cup whipping cream
½ cup vermouth (or any dry wine)
½ cup toasted pecans, slivered
1 large can mushrooms, sliced

Marinate shrimp in lemon juice and oil. Refrigerate. Cook rice according to directions on box. Sauté bell pepper and onion in 2 tablespoons butter. Add salt and pepper. Place in mixing bowl and add soup, cream, vermouth, pecans, mushrooms, rice, and drained shrimp. Place in baking dish and bake at 350 degrees F until heated thoroughly.

Stew

Andrea Hollander Budy

At 4 P.M., while her ex is sitting
in his easy chair somewhere in the grey
of his Iowa landscape, his desk high

with obligations, the unread
Sunday papers piled by his feet,
the winds faint, the traffic fainter,

the snowless cold out every
window of his house, and light
thrown through the clouds,

she will be standing at the kitchen sink
of her too familiar house, scraping
vegetables for stew and looking

out at the same bleak sky, paring
carrot peels into the sink, then potato,
letting them pile there like spent

snake skins. If only he
would open this door, how different
the falling of the light,

how autumn, not winter, the stew.

$\mathscr{B}$EEF STEW FOR ANY SEASON

1½ pounds stew meat, cut in
    2-inch pieces
1 tablespoon oil
water
1 tablespoon lemon juice
1 onion, sliced
2 beef bouillon cubes
3 stalks celery, diced
4 carrots, sliced
4 potatoes, cut in pieces
salt and pepper to taste

Brown meat on all sides in hot oil, turning frequently. Cover
with 1½ to 2 cups of water, lemon juice, sliced onion, and
bouillon cubes. Simmer for about an hour, covered. Add
other vegetables, salt, and pepper, and cook 30 to 40 minutes,
or until vegetables are tender.

Mother-daughter
small talk . . .
snap beans

Peggy Lyles

TONGUE-TIED

Naomi Shihab Nye

Someone just told me
our taste buds die
as we grow older.
They die one-by-one,
or in groups.
A child has whole galaxies.
We're lucky by now to retain a few.

This is why a child cries
if something tastes bad.

All day I walk around
opening and closing
my mouth.

The tortilla becomes a deeper tortilla.
The blackberry, packaged in its
    small square crypt,
reaches all the way back to its bush
for me, for what is left of me,
this dissolving kingdom
between my teeth.

$\mathcal{T}$ORTILLAS TO TEMPT YOUR TASTE BUDS

4 flour tortillas (found in refrigerator section
   of supermarket)
¾ block cream cheese (8-ounce size)
1 heaping tablespoon mayonnaise
1 tablespoon red bell pepper,
   finely chopped
1 tablespoon green olives, finely chopped
1 tablespoon shallots, finely chopped
⅓ pound ham, paper thin

Soften each tortilla by grilling in an ungreased
skillet over medium heat for 15 seconds. Mix
cream cheese with mayonnaise, red bell pepper,
olives, and shallots. Spread in thin layer over sur-
face of tortilla. Cover with layer of ham. Roll very
tightly and slice into pinwheels. Makes about 3½
dozen. Watch them disappear!

Making Bread

Dorothy Coffin Sussman

She counted those days among the best.
Nutty fragrance of rising dough, the humid southern air,
her body spreading out, gathering, filling up
at last. Earlier that month she painted the kitchen
yellow and took herself out of the dark.
Perched on countertops, barefoot (she laughed out loud),
she sang along with the radio and by herself laid a new floor
while the baby danced inside her.

She planted a grapefruit seed then and told herself,
no one else, that this was for her unborn child.
As long as it grew, so would the child.
A dozen years later, the seed is a tree,
a head taller than her son, its spindly arms
covered with thorns, a sharpness that takes her by surprise.

Today, she stops her kneading and buries her face in green leaves.
The faint citrus smell stays on her skin, and she wonders,
again and for the millionth time, how much luck
is involved, what will grow and what will not,
how a lush green curls out of the hard seed,
belly hard, the vagaries of heat, the right moment
for ripening. Dough on the rise, voluptuous,
fills the aluminum bowl, and she hugs it to herself,
dances around the room, around the room and around.

$\mathcal{S}$ALLY LUNN BREAD

½ cup real butter
⅓ cup sugar
4 cups sifted flour (plain)
1 cup lukewarm milk
1 teaspoon salt
3 eggs
1 package yeast

Cream butter and sugar. Add other ingredients. Beat with a wooden spoon. Let rise until double in bulk, 1-½ to 2 hours. Pour in well-buttered tube pan. Let rise again to double, 40 minutes to 1 hour. Bake 45 minutes at 350 degrees F.

$\int$PONGE CAKE

Ann Ritter

The four o'clock whistle brought them—Bett, Jean, Edna—
daily with gifts to Mother's kitchen. Born as daughters,
reluctantly they would play the role of wives.

Round, oil-clothed table bound them tight as a web
to her fallen bosom. Strong coffee
washed down afternoons, orange sponge cake, jelly rolls,
sweets to soak their days' bad news,
fuel to travel to domestic chores.

Then, young insects hearing some ancient, inborn signal,
at five they rose, borne on wind, with car keys, purses,
home to husbands, simple suppers.

$\mathscr{O}$ RANGE SPONGE CAKE

4 eggs
2 cups sugar
2 cups cake flour
2 teaspoons baking powder
pinch of salt
2 teaspoons orange extract
grated rind of one orange
1 cup milk
2 tablespoons butter

Preheat oven to 350 degrees F. Beat 4 eggs until
light. Add sugar and continue beating. Mix
together flour, baking powder, and salt. Beat into
egg mixture. Add orange extract and orange rind.
Heat milk and butter to almost boiling point.
Quickly stir into other ingredients. Bake in an
ungreased 10-inch tube pan for 45 minutes. Cool
in pan upside down over a bottle. Gently loosen
cake from pan with spatula before turning out on
serving plate.

OLD GEORGIA TEA CAKES

1 cup vegetable shortening
1 cup sugar
2 eggs, beaten
3 cups all-purpose flour
¼ teaspoon nutmeg
1 teaspoon baking powder

Cream shortening and sugar. Add beaten eggs. Sift together flour, nutmeg, and baking powder. Mix well into other ingredients and chill. Roll out thinly and cut with biscuit cutter. Bake at 375 degrees F for about ten minutes.

half a heart shape
in the handle—
steaming cup

Peggy Lyles

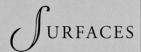URFACES

John Foster West

The first snow is powdered sugar
sprinkled over knobs and ridges, lumps in the cake
your microscopic eyes measure outward.
Yesterday's firm footing shimmers through,
giving contour and substance to a surface like gauze.
Somewhere down the immediate valley
an oscillating fan blasts across the face
of a cake of ice, to buffet you
and remind you of cold time,
while overhead an eggshell lid
covers you, fragile enough to crack
at your first sneeze.
Nearby, a pragmatic robin skips along
barely ahead of his snowshoe trail,
pausing now and then to peck holes
in the surface of his world.

$\mathcal{A}$UNT CLYDE'S CHOCOLATE LAYER CAKE

1 cup butter or margarine
2 cups sugar
4 eggs
3 cups sifted all-purpose flour
2 teaspoons baking powder
pinch of salt
1 cup milk
½ teaspoon vanilla
½ teaspoon lemon extract

Cream butter and sugar. Beat in eggs. Mix flour, baking powder, and salt. Add alternately with milk. Add flavorings. Bake in two 9-inch greased and floured pans at 350 degrees F for 30 to 35 minutes.

CHOCOLATE FROSTING

3 squares (1-ounce each)
   unsweetened chocolate, melted
⅓ cup soft butter or margarine
⅛ teaspoon salt
3 cups XXXX confectioner's sugar
¼ cup milk
1½ teaspoons vanilla

Add butter to melted chocolate. Mix in other ingredients until smooth and creamy. Add more sugar to thicken or milk to thin frosting if needed for a good spreading consistency.

TO A WASP

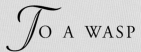

Janice

Townley

Moore

You must have chortled
finding that tiny hole
in the kitchen screen. Right
into my cheesecake batter
you dived,
no chance to swim ashore,
no saving spoon,
the mixer whirring
your legs, wings, stinger,
churning you into such
delicious death.
Never mind the bright April day.
Did you not see
rising out of cumulus clouds
that fist aimed at both of us?

ℬLACK FOREST CHEESECAKE ("LITE")

CRUST
1¼ cups chocolate cookie crumbs
3 tablespoons sugar
¼ cup margarine, melted

Mix all ingredients and press into a springform pan. Bake at 375 degrees F for 5 minutes. Cool.

CAKE
4 packages light cream cheese (8-ounce size)
1 cup sugar
2 large egg whites
1 teaspoon almond flavoring
2 tablespoons cornstarch
1 cup no-fat sour cream

Beat cream cheese with sugar until fluffy. Add egg whites, almond flavoring, and cornstarch and beat several minutes. Fold in sour cream and pour into crust. Bake at 450 degrees F for 10 minutes. Reduce heat to 200 degrees F and bake for 45 minutes. Turn off oven. Leave cake in oven with door cracked for 3 hours.

TOPPING
nondairy whipped topping
1 21-ounce can dark sweet cherry pie filling
        (add a few drops of red food coloring)
shaved or grated semisweet chocolate

Make a narrow border of nondairy whipped topping around outer edge. Spread cherry pie filling inside, but not close to center of cake. Use another border of whipped topping to enclose a generous amount of shaved chocolate in middle of cake.

$\mathcal{P}$EACH CUSTARD PIE

½ package (7-ounce size)
  sun-dried peaches
1 tablespoon sugar
2 cups milk, heated
3 eggs
¾ cup sugar
pinch of salt
½ teaspoon vanilla
½ teaspoon lemon extract
1 pie shell
butter

Cook dried peaches in water until soft. Drain. Mash with fork and sprinkle with 1 tablespoon of sugar. Heat milk and add eggs, sugar, salt, and flavorings. Line pie shell with layer of peaches. Pour custard mixture over peaches. Dot with thin slices of butter. Place pie on cookie sheet. Bake 15 minutes at 450 degrees F. Reduce heat to 350 degrees F and bake until a silver knife inserted comes out clean. Serve warm.

**EACHES**

Peter Davison

A mouthful of language to swallow:
stretches of beach, sweet clinches
breaches in walls, pleached branches;
britches hauled over haunches;
hunched leeches, wrenched teachers.
What English can do: ransack
the warmth that chuckles beneath
fuzzed surfaces, smooth velvet
richness, plashy juices.
I beseech you, peach,
clench me into the sweetness
of your reaches.

A C K N O W L E D G M E N T S

Grateful acknowledgment is made to the following publications
which first published some of the material in this book:

House Without a Dreamer (Story Line Press, 1993) for "Stew" under the title "Soup" by
Andrea Hollander Budy; *The Girl in the Midst of the Harvest* (Texas Tech University
Press, 1986) © by Kathryn Stripling Byer for "Potatoes" by Kathryn Stripling Byer;
Ms., Vol. II, No. 5, April 1992 for "Vegetable Market: Trying to Talk with a Friend" by
Mary Ann Coleman; *The Great Ledge* (Alfred A. Knopf, 1989) © 1989 by Peter
Davison for "Peaches" by Peter Davison, reprinted by permission of Alfred A Knopf
Inc; *Georgia Journal*, Vol. 13, No. 3, September 1993 for "Soufflé" by Blanche Flanders
Farley; *Georgia Journal*, Vol. 13, No. 3, September 1993 for "Afterward" by Judy
Goldman; *Frontiers: A Journal of Women Studies*, Vol. IX, No. 3, 1987 for "Eating Small
Birds" © by Sarah Gordon; *The Long Approach* (Viking, 1985) © 1985 by Maxine
Kumin for "Appetite" by Maxine Kumin; *High/Coo*, Vol. 5, No. 20, May 1981 for "her
sure hand" by Peggy Lyles; *Modern Haiku*, Vol. XIV, No. 3, Fall 1983 and *The Rise and
Fall of Sparrows, A Collection of North American Haiku* (Los Hombres Press, 1990) for
"Mother-daughter" by Peggy Lyles; *Haiku Quarterly*, Vol. 3, No. 3, Autumn 1991 (Best
of Issue Award) for "old homeplace" by Peggy Lyles; *Northeast*, Series V, No. 8, Spring
and Summer 1993 for "half a heartshape" by Peggy Lyles; *Habersham Review*, Vol. 13,
No. 2, Autumn 1994 for "Sustenance" by Judson Mitcham; *Light Year '85* (Bits Press,
1985) for "To a Wasp" © by Janice Townley Moore; *Light*, Vol. 1, No. 2, 1992 for "Julia
Child's Duck" by Janice Townley Moore; *Red Suitcase* (BOA Editions, Ltd., 1994) for
"Tongue-tied" © by Naomi Shihab Nye; *Georgia Journal*, Vol. 13, No. 3, September
1993 for "Homage to a Cook" by Rena G. Patton; *Georgia Journal*, Vol. 14, No. 2, 1994
for "Sponge Cake" by Ann Ritter; *Camaraderie* (1988) and *Wild Ginger* (Imagery Press,
1989) for "Seaoats" © by Bettie Sellers; "Love Poem at a Particular Breakfast for No
Particular Woman," reprinted with permission of Louisiana State University Press from
In All This Rain by John Stone, © 1980 by John Stone; *Georgia Journal*, Vol. 9, No. 1,
Spring 1989 for "Making Bread" by Dorothy Coffin Sussman; *Poets On:*, Vol. 9, No. 1,
Winter 1985 for "Your Poems Have Been Lost in the Mail" by Memye Curtis Tucker;
Poetry and Not Just Any Death (BOA Editions, 1979) for "Preserves" by Michael
Waters; and *Wry Wine* (J. F. Blair, 1977) for "Surfaces" by John Foster West.

ABOUT THE EDITORS

BLANCHE FLANDERS FARLEY is a librarian at the Atlanta History Center. She has an MA in art from the University of Michigan, an MFA in writing from Warren Wilson College, Swannanoa, North Carolina, and an MLS from Clark-Atlanta University in Atlanta, Georgia. A group of her poems were set to music in 1988, and one of her short stories won a PEN Syndicated Fiction Award in 1984. Her work has been published in literary journals, as well as anthologies and textbooks. A native of Wrightsville, Georgia, she lives in Atlanta.

JANICE TOWNLEY MOORE teaches English at Young Harris College in the mountains of northern Georgia. She has an MA in English from Auburn University, Auburn, Alabama. Her poetry has been included in nationally recognized magazines, literary journals, and anthologies, including *When I Am an Old Woman I Shall Wear Purple* (Papier-Mache Press, 1987). She is poetry editor for *Georgia Journal* and is a member of the North Carolina Writers' Network and the Georgia State Poetry Society. A native of Atlanta, she lives in Hayesville, North Carolina.

Fans of Deidre Scherer's exquisite fabric-and-thread images will enjoy her book, Threads of Experience, *featuring full-color reproductions of 25 artworks plus poetry and prose, selected by Sandra Haldeman Martz.*

P A P I E R - M A C H E P R E S S

At Papier-Mache Press, it is our goal to identify and successfully present important social issues through enduring works of beauty, grace, and strength. Through our work we hope to encourage empathy and respect among diverse communities, creating a bridge of understanding between the mainstream audience and those who might not otherwise be heard.

We appreciate you, our customer, and strive to earn your continued support. We also value the role of the bookseller in achieving our goals. We are especially grateful to the many independent booksellers whose presence ensures a continuing diversity of opinion, information, and literature in our communities. We encourage you to support these bookstores with your patronage.

We publish many fine books about women's experiences. We also produce lovely posters and T-shirts that complement our anthologies. Please ask your local bookstore which Papier-Mache items they carry. To receive our complete catalog, send your request to Papier-Mache Press, 135 Aviation Way, #14, Watsonville, CA 95076, or call our toll-free number, 800-927-5913.